DISCOVERING Space

STARS AND GALAXIES

Ian Graham

W

FRANKLIN WATTS
LONDON•SYDNEY

An Appleseed Editions book

First published in 2007 by Franklin Watts

Franklin Watts
338 Euston Road, London NW1 3BH

Franklin Watts Australia
Level 17/207 Kent St, Sydney, NSW 2000

© 2007 Appleseed Editions

Appleseed Editions Ltd
Well House, Friars Hill, Guestling, East Sussex TN35 4ET

Created by Q2A Creative
Series Editor: Honor Head
Designers: Diksha Khatri, Ashita Murgai
Picture Researchers: Lalit Dalal, Jyoti Sachdev

ISBN   978 0 7496 7549 3

Dewey classification: 523.8

All words in **bold** can be found in the glossary on page 30.

A CIP catalogue for this book is available from the British Library.

Picture credits
t: top, b: bottom, l: left, r: right, m: middle, c: centre
Cover images: Nasa: l, tr, NOAO: br,
Small images: The SINGG Survey Team and NOAO/ AURA/ NSF: cl, S. Points, C. Smith, R. Leiton,
C. Aguilera and NOAO/ AURA/ NSF: cm, Gemini Observatory/ Travis Rector, University of Alaska Anchorage/ NOAO: cr,
Peter Arnold Images Inc/ Photolibrary: 4b, Photo Researchers, Inc./ Photolibrary: 4-5 (background), Nasa/ ESA/ STScI: 6b,
Science Photo Library/ Photolibrary: 6t, 11b, 12b, 13b, 17b, 21t, 26b, 27b, Nasa: 7 (background), 9b, 10b, 14-15 (background),
15b, 19t, 19b, 20b, 21b, Steve Cannistra: 8b, William Attard McCarthy/ Shutterstock: 8-9 (background),
Nasa/ JPL-Caltech/ O. Krause: 11t, Historical Picture Archive/ Corbis: 13t, Robert Gendler/ Nasa: 14b,
Nasa/ JPL-Caltech/ R. Hurt: 16b, Gemini Observatory/ NOAO: 18b, 23b, 25b, Roger Ressmeyer/ Corbis: 22b,
European Space Agency: 23t, ESO: 24b, NASA/ JPL: 25t, Michael Knight/ Istockphoto: 27t.

Printed in China

Franklin Watts is a division of Hachette Children's Books

Contents

The night sky   4

Birth of a star   6

Star colours   8

Star death   10

Constellations   12

Galaxies   14

The Milky Way   16

Space clouds   18

The Big Bang   20

Star gazing   22

Solar systems   24

Searching for aliens   26

Timeline   28

Glossary   30

Index   32

The night sky

At night the sky is full of twinkling points of light. Nearly all of these are stars. Many of them are like our star, the **Sun**. They look much smaller than the Sun because they are so far away.

Rising and setting

As the Earth spins, the stars rise in the east, cross the sky and set in the west. Long ago sailors learned how to use the positions of well-known stars to steer their ships. Scientists have studied the stars for thousands of years, but we are still learning about them today.

On a clear night, you can see about 2,000 stars in the sky.

When you look at the stars, you are seeing light that has crossed **billions** of kilometres of space.

Clusters of stars

Stars are not spread evenly throughout the **Universe**. They gather together in giant clusters called galaxies. A **galaxy** contains **billions** of stars travelling through space, held together by **gravity**. Everywhere **astronomers** look in the sky, they find more and more galaxies. There are billions of galaxies and each galaxy contains billions of stars.

Closest stars

Name of star	Distance from Earth
Sun	0.000016 light years
Proxima centauri	4.24 light years
Alpha centauri A	4.35 light years
Alpha centauri B	4.35 light years
Barnard's star	5.98 light years
Wolf 359	7.78 light years
Lalande 21185	8.26 light years
Sirius A	8.55 light years
Sirius B	8.55 light years
Luyten 726-8A	8.73 light years

Spotlight on space

Long distances are usually measured in kilometres. But the distances between stars are so big that they are measured in units called light years. A light year is the distance light travels in one year, or nearly ten million million kilometres.

Birth of a star

There was a time when each of the stars that shines in the night sky did not exist. Stars have been forming for billions of years and new stars are still being born today. Stars form in vast clouds of gas and dust called **nebulae** that drift through space. Scientists can see these clouds and study the stars being formed in them.

The four biggest stars seen here are still very young – only a few hundred thousand years old.

Gas balls

Inside a gas cloud, gravity pulls together some of the gas to form thick clumps. These clumps pull more gas on to them. The clumps slowly grow bigger and bigger. As each clump grows, the gas at its centre is squashed harder and begins to heat up.

These stars are forming in giant pillars of gas and dust in the Eagle nebula.

A gas cloud starts to make new stars when a dying star explodes and sends gas rushing into it. Waves of gas push into the cloud and squash parts of it. Then gravity takes over and the formation of the new stars begins.

The Orion nebula is a gas cloud in which new stars are forming.

Star light

As a new star grows and heats up, it is hidden inside the cloud in which it formed. Eventually, the centre of the new star reaches several million degrees Celsius. Particles of matter smash into each other so hard that they stick together, or fuse, and give out a burst of energy. This is called nuclear fusion and when it begins, the star starts to give out light.

Orion nebula facts

Size	▶	30 light years
Distance from Earth	▶	1,500 light years away

Star colours

Stars look like identical pinpoints of light, but there are many differences between them. Some are **dwarf stars** no bigger than Earth. Others are supergiants 1,000 times bigger than the Sun – and there are even stars that pulse like heartbeats.

The colour of heat

The Sun is yellow because it is so hot. Its surface temperature is 5,500 degrees Celsius. Stars hotter than the Sun are white, blue or violet. Stars which are cooler than the Sun are orange or red.

The Pleiades, or Seven Sisters, is a cluster of young, hot stars.

Star colour facts	
Colour of star	**Temperature**
Violet	more than 28,000 °C
Blue	7,500–28,000 °C
Blue-white	6,000–7,500 °C
White-yellow	5,000–6,000 °C
Orange-red	3,500–5,000 °C
Red	less than 3,500 °C

Spotlight on
space

More than half the stars in the sky are not on their own, like the Sun. They are actually in pairs and orbit around each other. Two stars orbiting each other are called a binary star.

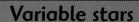

Variable stars

Stars that change in brightness are called **variable stars**. Some variable stars grow brighter and dimmer because they actually grow and shrink. Sometimes a star suddenly becomes 10,000 times brighter than before. This is a **nova**. It happens when one star pulls gas off another star. The extra gas piles up on the star and explodes in a dazzling flash.

Mira, in the far-off **constellation** Cetus, was the first variable star to be discovered. These pictures show how its brightness varies.

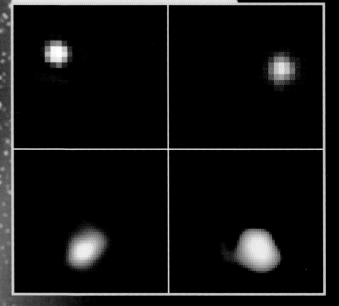

Most of the stars in the night sky are too dim to be seen without a telescope.

Star death

A star may shine for billions of years but eventually it will run out of the fuel it needs to keep shining. What happens then depends on how big it is. It might just fade away or it might blow itself to bits.

The smallest stars

When a star like the Sun begins to run out of **hydrogen**, it swells up to form a huge star called a **red giant**. In time, its outer layers of hot gas drift away into space. All that is left behind is a tiny star called a **white dwarf**. A white dwarf is made of matter that is so tightly packed together that just a teaspoonful would weigh a tonne. White dwarfs keep cooling down and dimming until they completely fade away.

Star size

Type of star		Size across the middle
The Sun	▷	1.4 million kilometres
A red giant	▷	up to 1,000 Suns
A white dwarf	▷	about the same size as the Earth
A neutron star	▷	about 20 kilometres

A red giant star is red because its outer layers cool down as the star grows bigger and glow red.

This is the shattered remains of a star that exploded in a **supernova** more than 340 years ago.

Spotlight on
space

When the biggest stars explode, they produce one of the strangest objects in the universe – a black hole. When the star's core collapses, its gravity is so strong that nothing can escape from it, not even light.

Flash, bang, pulse!

Stars much bigger than the Sun collapse so powerfully that they tear themselves to bits in a dazzling explosion called a supernova. All that is left is a tiny spinning core called a **neutron star** which sends out narrow beams of radio waves. If they sweep past Earth, the star seems to have a throbbing pulse. This is called a pulsating star, or **pulsar**.

A supernova blasts stardust in all directions.

Constellations

For thousands of years, people who studied the stars divided them up into groups called constellations. Astronomers still use constellations today, as a map to find their way around the sky.

Naming the constellations

Many of the constellations astronomers use today were named thousands of years ago by astronomers in the Middle East and ancient Greece. The ancient astronomers thought that groups of stars looked like an animal, or a person or creature from mythology, so they named them after it.

Drawings around the stars in constellations show how they look like their name. This is Capricorn the goat.

Zodiac constellation names

Name		Shape
Aries	▶	ram
Taurus	▶	bull
Gemini	▶	twins
Cancer	▶	crab
Leo	▶	lion
Virgo	▶	girl
Libra	▶	scales
Scorpio	▶	scorpion
Sagittarius	▶	archer
Capricorn	▶	goat
Aquarius	▶	water carrier
Pisces	▶	fish

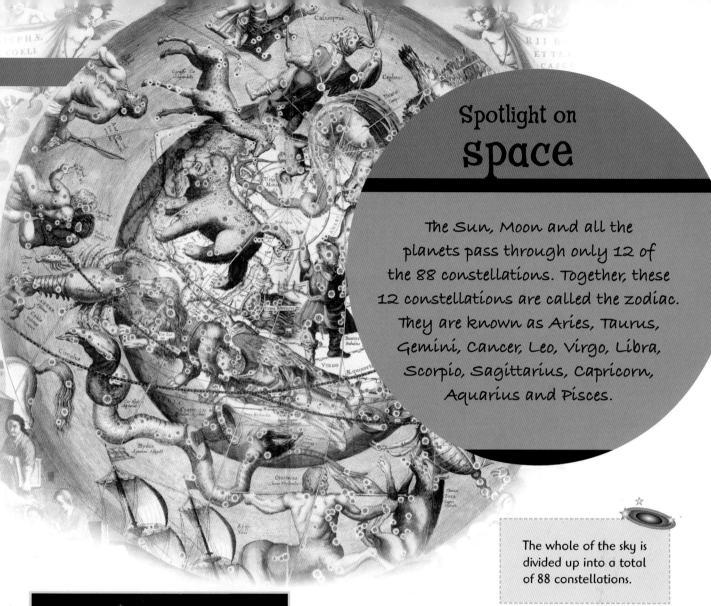

Spotlight on
space

The Sun, Moon and all the planets pass through only 12 of the 88 constellations. Together, these 12 constellations are called the zodiac. They are known as Aries, Taurus, Gemini, Cancer, Leo, Virgo, Libra, Scorpio, Sagittarius, Capricorn, Aquarius and Pisces.

The whole of the sky is divided up into a total of 88 constellations.

Ancient constellations

The stars in a constellation are not usually close together. Some of them are much further away from Earth than other stars in the same constellation. They appear to be close together when we look up into the night sky but they are light years apart.

The constellation Orion is named after the great hunter from the myths of ancient Greece.

Galaxies

Galaxies are huge collections of stars moving through space together. They come in many different shapes and sizes. The smallest galaxies may contain just a few million stars. The biggest have hundreds of billions of stars.

Spinning in space

The stars in a galaxy pull each other together but they do not fall into the centre of the galaxy because the whole galaxy is spinning. The spinning motion tries to fling the stars apart. This is balanced by gravity, which tries to pull the stars together.

Andromeda facts

Size	▶	160,000 light years across
Number of stars	▶	400 billion
Distance from Earth	▶	2.4 million light years

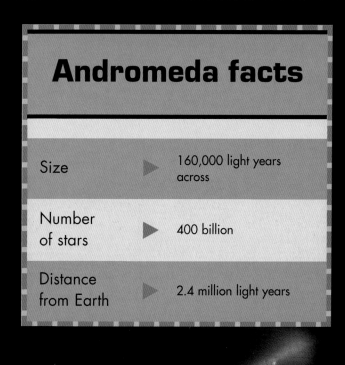

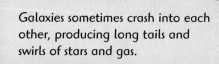

Galaxies sometimes crash into each other, producing long tails and swirls of stars and gas.

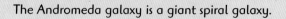

The Andromeda galaxy is a giant spiral galaxy.

Spotlight on
space

Some galaxies are much brighter than we expect them to be. They are called quasars. Scientists think their extra light is given out by stars and gas just before they fall into a gigantic black hole at the centre of the galaxy.

Interesting shapes

Most galaxies are elliptical in shape – the shape of a rugby ball. Some galaxies are spirals. They have long swirls of stars and gas curling away from a ball of stars in the middle. More than a third of all galaxies have no definite shape. These are called irregular galaxies.

Some spiral galaxies have a straight bar of stars, dust and gas across the middle.

The Milky Way

Earth is part of a galaxy called the Milky Way. If we could look at our galaxy from above, we would see that the Milky Way is a spiral galaxy. It contains about 200 billion stars.

Old and young

The stars in the bulge in the middle of the Milky Way are older than the stars in the spiral arms. The arms contain a lot of gas and dust where new stars are still forming. Earth is in one of the galaxy's spiral arms.

Milky Way facts

Size	▶	up to 100,000 light years across
Central bulge	▶	15,000 light years across 6,000 light years thick
Number of stars	▶	about 200 billion

Spiral arms

Central bulge

Our galaxy, the Milky Way, is a spiral galaxy.

Spotlight on
space

The centre of our galaxy is a mystery, hidden behind clouds of dust. Scientists think there is a massive black hole there. More than two million Suns may have fallen into it. But do not worry, there is no danger of Earth falling in!

The Local Group

Our galaxy is one of a cluster of galaxies that travel through space together, called the Local Group. There are about 40 galaxies in the Local Group. Clusters of galaxies sometimes combine with other clusters to form a supercluster. The Local Group belongs to a supercluster called the Local Supercluster.

The centre of the Milky Way may look like this, with stars and gas shining brightly as they spiral into a black hole.

Space clouds

Galaxies contain vast clouds of gas and dust called nebulae. Some nebulae are places where new stars are made. Other nebulae are the remains of old, dying and dead stars.

Light and dark

Some nebulae are bright and easy to see. They are lit up by nearby stars. Other nebulae are dustier, darker and harder to see. They show up as a dark shadow if there is a bigger, brighter nebula behind them.

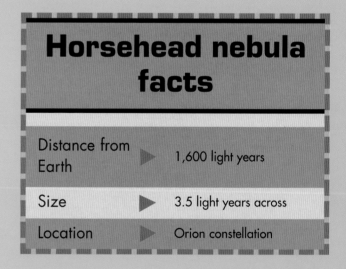

Horsehead nebula facts

Distance from Earth	1,600 light years
Size	3.5 light years across
Location	Orion constellation

This dusty, dark nebula is called the Horsehead nebula because of its shape.

Fuzzy planets or stars?

More than 200 years ago, astronomers discovered tiny, fuzzy discs of light in the sky. They looked a bit like planets through a telescope, so they were called planetary nebulae, but they have nothing to do with planets. They are actually old stars that have blown lots of their gas out into space.

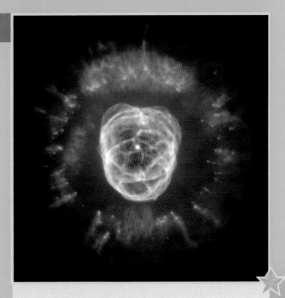

This planetary nebula is called the Eskimo nebula because it looks like a face inside a furry hood.

Spotlight on
space

The gas and dust in a nebula are spread very thinly through space. If you could collect all the gas and dust from an area 1,000 kilometres long, 1,000 kilometres wide and 1,000 kilometres high, it would weigh only one kilogram!

All nebula are made mostly of hydrogen.

The Big Bang

Did the Universe have a beginning or has it been here forever? Scientists had different ideas about this in the past but today, most scientists think the Universe began nearly 14 billion years ago in a gigantic explosion called the **Big Bang**.

Cooling down

Moments after the Big Bang, the temperature of the Universe was about 1,000 million degrees Celsius. It has been cooling down ever since. A satellite called *COBE* (the *Cosmic Background Explorer*) made a map of the warmth left over from the Big Bang.

COBE mission

Launched	▶	1989
Orbit	▶	900 kilometres above the ground
Length of mission	▶	4 years
Mission ended	▶	1993

The *COBE* satellite **scanned** the whole sky every six months

Heat shield protects instruments

Solar panels produce electricity

Radio antenna

Within a few seconds of the Big Bang, the first particles of matter began to form. A few hundred thousand years later, the first stars lit up the young Universe.

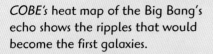

Space and time began when the Big Bang happened.

COBE's heat map of the Big Bang's echo shows the ripples that would become the first galaxies.

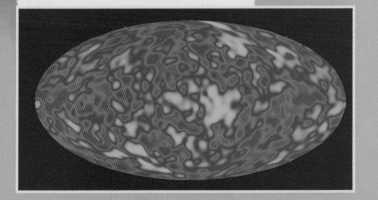

Flying apart

The Universe has been growing ever since the Big Bang. Scientists thought gravity was acting like a brake and slowing this down. They even thought that gravity might stop the Universe growing and make it collapse again in a Big Crunch. Now astronomers have discovered that the galaxies are flying apart faster and faster, but no one understands why.

Star gazing

The stars and galaxies are so far away that we cannot visit them, or send space probes to explore them. Scientists study them by using telescopes on Earth and in space which collect the light and other energy that they give out.

Twinkle, twinkle

Stars seem to twinkle because the light they send bends as it travels through the Earth's **atmosphere**. Twinkling makes it difficult to take clear pictures of stars so telescopes are built above the thickest part of the Earth's atmosphere, on top of mountains. From here they can get a clearer view of the stars.

Spotlight on
space

Radio telescopes make pictures from radio waves instead of light. Planets, stars, galaxies and gas clouds all give out radio waves. A radio telescope usually has a big metal dish to collect lots of radio waves.

Modern astronomical telescopes have a huge curved mirror to collect starlight.

Space telescopes

The Earth's atmosphere blocks some of the energy given out by stars. Telescopes on Earth cannot receive it but telescopes in space can study all the energy given out by stars and galaxies. Some space telescopes make pictures from invisible **ultraviolet rays**. Others receive **infrared rays** or X-rays. The Hubble Space Telescope makes pictures from light.

Solar panel

Cameras and instruments

Light enters here

Radio antenna

The Hubble Space Telescope orbits the Earth about 600 kilometres above the ground.

The telescopes of the Mauna Kea **Observatory** in Hawaii are built on top of a sleeping volcano.

Hubble Space Telescope facts

Length	▶	13 metres
Diameter	▶	up to 4.2 metres
Weight	▶	11.6 tonnes
Primary mirror	▶	2.4 metres across

Solar systems

The Sun is not the only star with planets orbiting it. There are planets orbiting other stars and these are called **extrasolar planets** or exoplanets. They are very hard to find because they are so far away and hidden in the bright light of the stars.

Alien giants

About 200 exoplanets have been found. Most of them are huge planets, even bigger than the giant of our **Solar System**, Jupiter. Scientists believe there are also exoplanets as small as Earth.

This is what a giant exoplanet orbiting a small star 200 light years from Earth might look like.

Exoplanet facts

First exoplanet found	▶ 1992
Closest exoplanet	▶ 63 light years away
Furthest exoplanet	▶ 21,500 light years away
Oldest exoplanet	▶ 13 billion years old

Finding planets

Exoplanets are hard to see, but the tug of their gravity as they orbit a star can make the star wobble. So a wobbling star may have planets. If a planet moves in front of a star, the star may look a little dimmer for a while. Even the dust around a star can show if there is a planet there – the planet's gravity can change the shape of the dust cloud.

The Terrestrial Planet Finder is an instrument being designed to search for Earth-sized planets orbiting other stars.

Kepler looks for dips in starlight caused by planets.

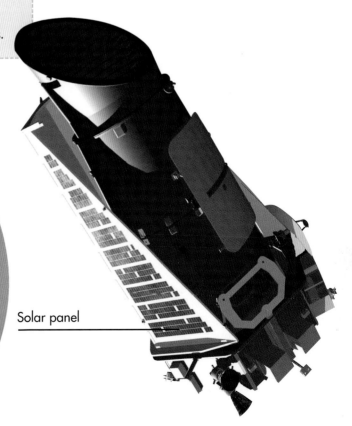

Spotlight on
space

A spacecraft called Kepler will be launched in 2008 to search for planets the same size as Earth. Its 95-centimetre telescope will watch 100,000 stars at the same time for any sign of small planets orbiting them.

Solar panel

Searching for aliens

People have wondered for thousands of years if we are alone in the Universe. So far, we have not found life on any other planet. But some scientists are studying stars for signs of intelligent beings on the planets orbiting them.

Is anybody out there?

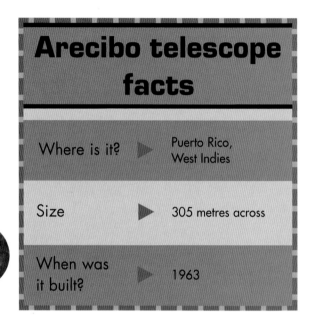

Looking for intelligent beings in space is called the Search For Extra-Terrestrial Intelligence (SETI). SETI scientists use radio telescopes to try to pick up radio signals from aliens.

Arecibo telescope facts

Where is it?	▶	Puerto Rico, West Indies
Size	▶	305 metres across
When was it built?	▶	1963

The Arecibo radio telescope is used to listen for alien radio messages.

This is an artist's idea of what an alien spacecraft might look like.

Help look for aliens

Radio signals picked up by a radio telescope are searched for anything that might have been sent by aliens. This job is done by computers. In fact, it is done by five million home computers in more than 200 countries. Anyone can help by joining the SETI@home project. You might find the next Wow! message.

Spotlight on
space

In 1977, SETI scientists received a radio signal from space. One scientist wrote 'Wow!' on the page of information where it was spotted. It is still known as the Wow! signal. No one knows if it was really from aliens.

SETI scientists study results from the Arecibo radio telescope.

Timeline

140 BC
The Greek astronomer Hipparchus produced the first known star catalogue, with accurate positions for about 800 stars.

c. AD 950
The Arab astronomer Abul-Husain al-Sufi produced a star catalogue. He is also the first person known to have seen the two brightest galaxies that can be seen without a telescope – the Andromeda Galaxy and the Large Magellanic Cloud.

1006
A brilliant supernova is seen in a constellation called Lupus.

1054
A brilliant supernova appears in the constellation Taurus. The remains of the star that blew itself apart are still visible today as the Crab nebula.

1572
A supernova explodes in the constellation Cassiopeia.

1612
The Orion nebula is discovered.

1802
The German-born astronomer William Herschel discovers binary stars.

1834
Astronomers discover that the star Sirius wobbles and work out that there must be another star orbiting it.

1838
The son of William Herschel, John Herschel, makes the first detailed survey of the far southern stars from southern Africa.

1845
Irish astronomer Lord Rosse builds the world's biggest telescope at Birr Castle in Ireland.

1863
Astronomers divide stars into different types according to their colours and temperatures.

1864
Astronomers discover that nebulae are made of gas.

1885
A supernova is seen in the Andromeda galaxy.

1901
A brilliant supernova is seen in the Perseus constellation.

1918
Astronomers work out the size of the Milky Way.

1923
American astronomer Edwin Hubble proves that the galaxies are outside the Milky Way.

1931
American scientists Karl Jansky discovers radio waves coming from space.

1937
American astronomer Grote Reber builds the first radio telescope.

1938
Scientists begin to work out what makes stars shine.

1955
The world's biggest radio telescope is built at Jodrell Bank in England.

1960
Construction of the Arecibo radio telescope begins on the island of Puerto Rico.

1963
The first quasars are discovered.

1967
British scientist Jocelyn Bell-Burnell discovers the first pulsar.

1974
A radio message is beamed from the Arecibo radio dish in the direction of a cluster of stars 25,000 light years away, so it will take 25,000 years to get there. If any aliens are there to receive it, a reply from them will take another 25,000 years to come back.

1977
Scientists pick up a radio signal that might have been sent by aliens.

1978
The *Einstein X-ray Observatory* is launched into space.

The *International Ultraviolet Explorer* satellite is launched.

1983
The *Infrared Astronomical Satellite (IRAS)* is launched.

1990
The Hubble Space Telescope is launched.

The *ROSAT X-ray* satellite is launched.

1991
The *Compton Gamma Ray Observatory* is launched into space to study distant explosions in space called gamma ray bursts.

1995
The *Infrared Space Observatory* is launched.

1996
The *Beppo-Sax X-ray* satellite is launched.

1999
The Chandra X-ray Telescope and Newton X-ray Telescope are launched to study objects in space, including pulsars and black holes.

2003
The Spitzer Infrared Space Telescope is launched to study cool objects in space, including cool stars, exoplanets and giant cool clouds of gas and dust.

2005
The first photograph is taken of a planet orbiting another star.

2008
Launch of the *Kepler* spacecraft to search for Earth-sized planets orbiting other stars.

2011
Launch of the James Webb Space Telescope.

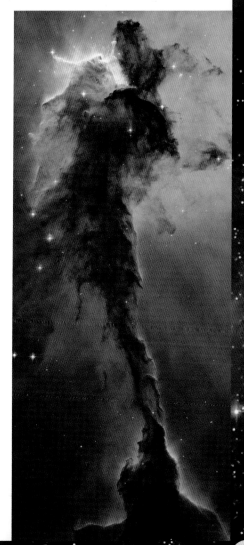

Glossary

astronomers Scientists who study astronomy.

atmosphere The gas around a planet or moon. The Earth's atmosphere is made of air.

Big Bang The explosion that brought the Universe into being nearly 14 billion years ago.

billions One thousand millions.

black hole An object in space with a pull of gravity so strong that not even light can escape from it.

constellation One of 88 groups of stars.

dwarf stars Small stars such as the Sun.

extrasolar planets Planets orbiting a star that is not the Sun. Also called exoplanets.

galaxy A collection of stars moving through space, held together by their pull of gravity.

gravity An invisible force that pulls things towards each other. Earth's gravity pulls us down on to the ground. The Sun's gravity holds the planets in their orbits.

hydrogen A colourless gas. Stars are mostly made of hydrogen.

infrared rays Energy waves longer than red light.

light years Units of measurement. One light year is the distance light travels in one year, or nearly ten million million kilometres.

mythology A collection of myths or stories usually about superhuman beings and their adventures.

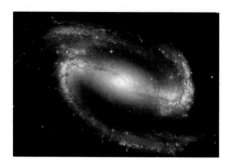

nebulae Clouds of gas and dust in space.

neutron star The tiniest type of star; the remains of a huge star that has exploded. It is called a neutron star because it is made of particles of matter called neutrons.

nova A star that has a sudden outburst of energy which makes it hundreds of thousands of times brighter for a short time.

observatory A building or buildings with telescopes for studying objects in the Universe.

orbit To travel around the Sun, a moon or a planet.

planets Very big objects in orbit around a star.

pulsar A spinning neutron star producing beams of radio waves that sweep past the Earth, giving the star a throbbing pulse.

quasar The dazzlingly bright centre of a distant galaxy, probably caused by stars and gas heating up before they fall into a black hole.

red giant A star that has swollen up and turned red because it has run out of hydrogen.

scanned Observed or studied closely.

Solar System The Sun, planets, moons and everything else that orbits the Sun, travelling through space together.

Sun The Earth's star, the star at the centre of our Solar System.

supernova A giant explosion that tears a massive star apart.

Universe All the space, matter, energy and everything else that exists anywhere.

variable stars Stars which can be brighter or darker.

white dwarf A star made of as much matter as the Sun, but which is as small as the Earth, formed when a star like the Sun reaches the end of its time.

zodiac The 12 constellations that the Sun, Moon and all the planets pass through.

ultraviolet rays Invisible rays that come from the Sun. It is these rays that burn our skin.

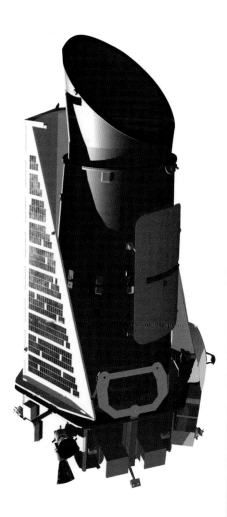

Index

Arecibo radio
   telescope 26, 27

Big Bang 20, 21
binary stars 9
black hole 11, 15, 17

COBE satellite 20, 21
constellations 9, 12, 13

exoplanets 24, 25

galaxies
  Andromeda 14
  Milky Way 16, 17
galaxy shape 14, 15

Hubble Space
   Telescope 23

Kepler spacecraft 25

light year 5
Local Group 17
Local Supercluster 17

Mauna Kea
  Observatory 23

nebulae 6, 7, 18, 19
neutron star 10, 11
nova 9
nuclear fusion 7

pulsar 11

quasar 15

radio telescopes 22, 26
red giant 10

(SETI) Search for Extra-
   Terrestrial Intelligence
   26, 27
star
  birth 6, 7
  colours 8, 9
  death 10, 11
  temperature 8
supernova 11

telescopes 22, 23
Terrestrial Planet
   Finder 25

variable star 9

white dwarf 10

WEBFINDER

http://www.bbc.co.uk/science/space/stars/index.shtml

http://www.bbc.co.uk/science/space/origins/bigbang/index.shtml

http://www.bbc.co.uk/science/space/deepspace/galaxy/index.shtml

http://spaceplace.nasa.gov/en/kids/cs_space.shtml

http://www.kidsastronomy.com/galaxys.htm

http://coolcosmos.ipac.caltech.edu//cosmic_kids/AskKids/galaxies.shtml

http://www.esa.int/esaKIDSen/Starsandgalaxies.html

http://www.space.kids.us/themilkyway.html